Northern sky

★ First Magnitude star
★ Second Magnitude star
★ Third Magnitude star

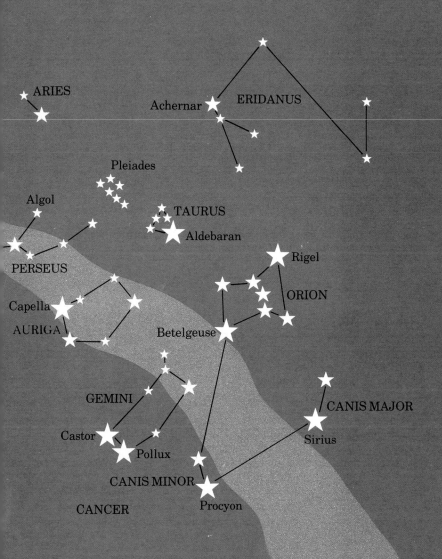

ARIES

Achernar ERIDANUS

Pleiades

Algol

TAURUS

Aldebaran

PERSEUS

Rigel

Capella

ORION

AURIGA

Betelgeuse

GEMINI

CANIS MAJOR

Castor

Sirius

Pollux

CANIS MINOR

CANCER

Procyon

LEO

Regulus

Jennifer

Credits

Feature illustrations

Terry Pastor pages 5 (bottom left), 6-7,
7 (left), 8-9 (top), 10, 10-11 (centre), 12,
17 (right), 24-25 (centre), 25, 27, 28-29,
31 (right), 33, 34-35, 38-39, cover
Tom Stimpson pages 3, 4-5 (centre),
14-15, 16-17 (centre), 19, 22-23,
30-31 (centre), 36-37, 37, title page,
end sheets

Additional illustrations

Jim Robins pages 11 (right), 16 (left),
20-21, 24 (left), 32
Elizabeth Wood pages 2, 5 (bottom right),
6 (left), 7 (right), 8-9 (bottom), 18, 30 (left), 40

Editor Wendy Boase
Designer Judith Escreet

Picture researcher Judy Lungen
Photography
page 4 Hale Observatory; page 11 Royal
Observatory, Edinburgh; page 13 Royal
Observatory, Edinburgh; page 15 NASA; page
20 Hale Observatory; page 24 JPL-NASA; page
26 (left) NASA/Space Frontiers, (right) NASA/
Geological Museum, London; page 29 NASA/
Geological Museum, London; page 32
JPL-NASA; page 35 Mt Wilson Observatory/
Geological Museum, London

Published 1981 by Methuen Children's Books Ltd,
11 New Fetter Lane, London EC4P 4EE
in association with
Walker Books, 17-19 Hanway House,
Hanway Place, London W1P 9DL

© 1981 Walker Books Ltd
First printed 1981
Printed and bound by
L.E.G.O., Vicenza, Italy

British Library Cataloguing in Publication Data
Ford, Adam
    Spaceship Earth. - (All about earth).
    1. Astronomy - Juvenile literature
    I. Title   II. Series
    520   QB46
    ISBN 0-416-05640-7

Contents

SPACESHIP EARTH

**Written by
Adam Ford**

Consultant Dr Gilbert Fielder
Head of Lunar and Planetary Unit
University of Lancaster

METHUEN/WALKER BOOKS
London · Sydney · Auckland · Toronto

The Earth

We live on a planet which travels silently and smoothly through space like a giant space ship. The universe surrounds us on all sides, and is above and below us.

The vastness of the universe
The amount of empty space in the universe is difficult for the mind to grasp. Imagine the Earth as a grapefruit 10cm in diameter. Then, on a scale model, the Sun would have to be a 10 metre-high bonfire 1km away. You would have to travel a quarter-of-a-million kilometres to light another bonfire to represent the nearest star.

Despite such vast distances, you don't need a telescope to enjoy astronomy. Astronomy is the study of the objects in the universe, all of which are moving in space just as the Earth does. Because the Earth has such a clear atmosphere, many objects in our sky can be seen with the naked eye.

Motion in space
Six months ago, Earth was on the far side of the Sun. It will be there again six months from now, because the planet orbits the Sun once a year, travelling at 30km per second. The Earth also spins on its axis once every 24 hours. We do not feel either of these movements, although they happen constantly.

All the objects we can see in our sky – the Sun, Moon, planets and stars – appear to move above us every day. Of course, this daily movement is an illusion. It is the Earth that is turning beneath the sky.

At the same time, the solar system (the Sun, the Earth and the eight other planets and their moons) is moving with the stars of our galaxy. The galaxy, or star system, is turning about its own centre, which gives the solar system an orbital velocity of approximately 250 km per second. But that is not all. Recently, it has been discovered that our galaxy itself is slowly falling through space. Slowly, that is, for a galaxy. We are tumbling towards a denser part of the universe at about 600 km per second. At that speed, you could cross the Atlantic Ocean in the time it takes to count to seven!

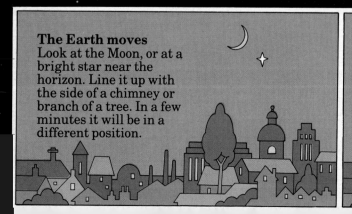

The Earth moves
Look at the Moon, or at a bright star near the horizon. Line it up with the side of a chimney or branch of a tree. In a few minutes it will be in a different position.

The Moon or star only appears to have moved. It is really the chimney or tree which has moved, along with the whole landscape, as the Earth spins on its axis.

Earth, accompanied by its Moon, moves through space at an astonishing speed. Although the Sun is 400 times the diameter of the Moon, both objects look roughly the same size because the Moon is much closer to us.

Our Sun

Earth has bathed in the Sun's heat and light for over 4,500 million years. Without the Sun, Earth could not have been formed and life would not have evolved on our planet.

The Sun is one of the smaller types of stars, and is sometimes referred to as a yellow dwarf. As stars go, the Sun is very unspectacular. Compared with the Earth, on the other hand, it is enormous. It would take more than one million worlds like ours to make an object the same size.

The Sun as a giant bomb

The Sun shines by releasing heat and light energy from hydrogen gas. But it is not burning the way fires burn on Earth. The Sun is exploding constantly, like a hydrogen bomb.

Deep in its interior, where the pressure and temperature are tremendous, a nuclear reaction is occurring. Hydrogen atoms are joining together to form helium, in a process called nuclear fusion. It is a process we hope to imitate on Earth, to provide energy.

The Sun 'burns up' 4 million tonnes of its material every second, and the temperature at its centre is about 20 million degrees Centigrade. The outer surface of the Sun (the photosphere which we can see) is much cooler – about 6,000°C.

It came as a shock to some people in 17th-century Europe, to discover that the Sun was not the perfect object they had imagined. It has spots. They appear in flushes which reach a peak in their cycle about every 11 years.

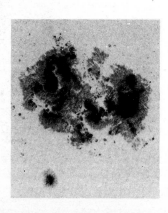

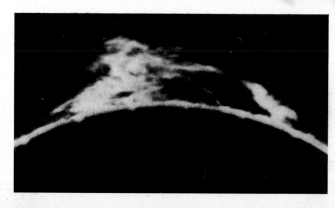

The temperature at the centre of a sunspot (left) is 4,000°C, while that of the Sun's surface is 6,000°C. The darkness of the spot is due to this temperature difference. Eruptions on the Sun's surface (right) may fling jets of gas hundreds of kilometres into space. These prominences, as they are called, travel at tremendous speeds.

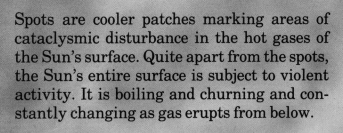

Sunspots are associated with intense magnetic 'storms'. At the peak of their 11-year cycle, some sunspots are many times bigger than the Earth. They may last a few days, or even several weeks.

Spots are cooler patches marking areas of cataclysmic disturbance in the hot gases of the Sun's surface. Quite apart from the spots, the Sun's entire surface is subject to violent activity. It is boiling and churning and constantly changing as gas erupts from below.

Trails of fire

Associated with sunspots are bright flares which throw great arches of matter thousands of kilometres into space. Electrically charged particles flung away from the Sun by these flares arrive at the Earth about a day later. They cause the upper atmosphere to glow. The result is a display of various colours: the Aurora Borealis in the northern hemisphere or Aurora Australis in the southern.

The Aurora Borealis, or Northern Lights. These curtains of vivid colour, which hang in the night sky, look as though they are being stirred gently by the wind.

Viewing the Sun
You can damage your eyes permanently if you look directly at the Sun with the naked eye, binoculars or a telescope. Focus the image of the Sun on to a sheet of white cardboard held about 30cm away from a telescope's eye-piece.

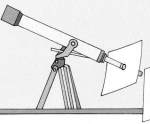

Light

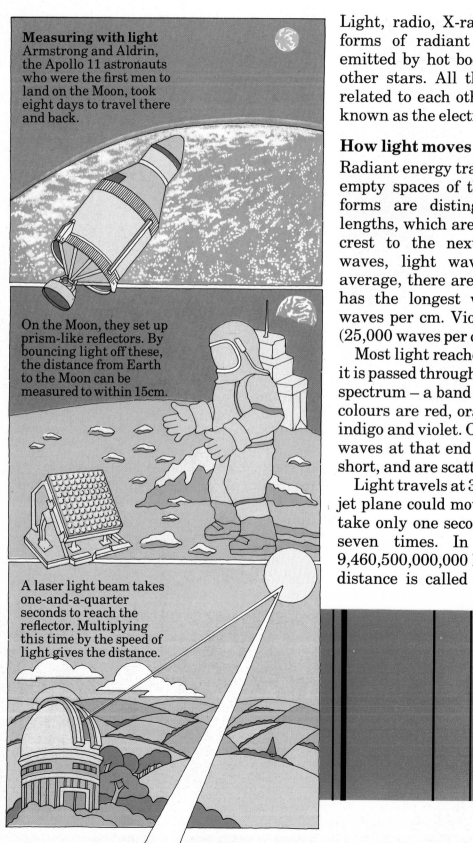

Measuring with light
Armstrong and Aldrin, the Apollo 11 astronauts who were the first men to land on the Moon, took eight days to travel there and back.

On the Moon, they set up prism-like reflectors. By bouncing light off these, the distance from Earth to the Moon can be measured to within 15cm.

A laser light beam takes one-and-a-quarter seconds to reach the reflector. Multiplying this time by the speed of light gives the distance.

Light, radio, X-rays and Gamma rays are forms of radiant energy. This energy is emitted by hot bodies such as the Sun and other stars. All these kinds of energy are related to each other, and make up what is known as the electromagnetic spectrum.

How light moves

Radiant energy travels in waves through the empty spaces of the universe. The various forms are distinguished by their wavelengths, which are measured from one wave crest to the next. Compared with radio waves, light waves are very short. On average, there are 17,000 per cm. Red light has the longest wavelength, with 12,500 waves per cm. Violet light has the shortest (25,000 waves per cm).

Most light reaches us as white light. When it is passed through a prism, it splits up into a spectrum – a band of individual colours. The colours are red, orange, yellow, green, blue, indigo and violet. Our sky is blue because the waves at that end of the spectrum are very short, and are scattered by the atmosphere.

Light travels at 300,000 km per second. If a jet plane could move at that speed, it would take only one second to fly round the world seven times. In a year, light travels 9,460,500,000,000 km. For convenience, this distance is called a light year. It is much

If light passes through a prism at an angle, it is refracted, or bent, and splits up into the colours of the spectrum.

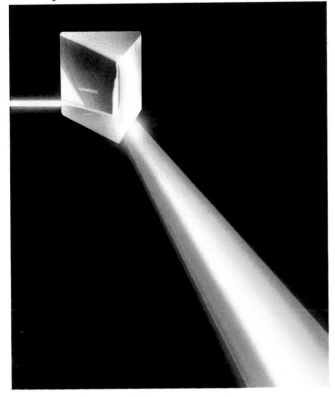

Colours in sunlight
You can see the colours of the spectrum if you catch sunlight in water. Put a mirror in the water at an angle, then reflect the colours on to a sheet of white cardboard held opposite. You will have to experiment to find the right positions for the card and the mirror.

easier to say that the nearest star, Proxima Centauri (companion star to Alpha Centauri), is four-and-a-quarter light years away, than it is to give the distance in kilometres.

What a spectrum reveals
Light comes to us directly from a hot body, or by reflection from colder ones such as the Moon, the planets or great clouds of inter-stellar gas called nebulae. As light leaves a star, some of it is re-absorbed by the outer atmosphere of that body. This results in dark absorption lines appearing across the spectrum. Astronomers know which materials absorb a particular wavelength, and they have learned a great deal about the composition of the Sun, stars and even distant galaxies from absorption lines.

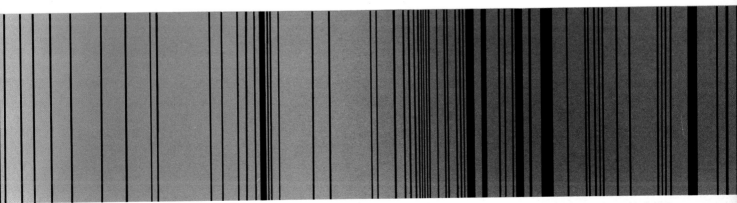

The dark lines on this absorption spectrum represent various gases which have absorbed the light as it left the surface of the Sun.

Gravity

If gravity suddenly ceased, the Sun and all the stars would explode instantly. The Earth would fly away from the Sun, which holds it in orbit, and rapidly begin to fall apart. The Moon would spin away from the Earth. The other planets would career off into the void and some would disintegrate.

A mysterious force

Every object or particle in the universe exerts a gravitational pull on all its neighbours. This is stated in the First Law of Gravitation, formulated in the 17th century by Isaac Newton. Although we know what gravity does, no one understands what it is. Gravity is a complete mystery. Experiments have been set up to try to detect gravity waves, if there are such things, but without success.

Scientists do know, however, that the greater the mass of an object, the stronger its pull of gravity. Mass is the amount of matter packed into an object, not simply its size. A car, for instance, can be crushed into a small cube, but the cube would still contain all the original matter. It would have the same mass (or be as 'massive') as the whole car. Weight, on the other hand, varies with the strength of the gravity that pulls upon the given mass.

The universal force
Newton worked out that gravity, the force which pulls an apple to Earth, is exerted by every object in the universe.

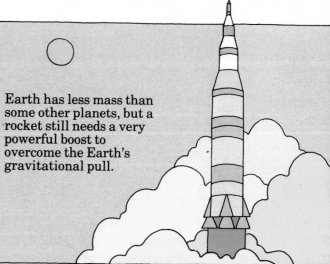

Earth has less mass than some other planets, but a rocket still needs a very powerful boost to overcome the Earth's gravitational pull.

Gravity controls our solar system. Without it, the Sun and stars would explode. All the planets would hurtle away into space. The Earth's seas would cascade from its surface as our planet began to disintegrate.

The Moon has less mass and weaker gravity than the Earth. Astronauts, weighing about 80kg on Earth, found they could bounce round on the Moon because there they weighed only about 13kg each. Yet the Moon has sufficient gravitational pull to attract the water of Earth's seas, and so cause the tides. On an asteroid, a lump of rock only a few kilometres across, gravity is so weak that an astronaut would feel as light as a feather.

Gravity in the universe

The Sun is massive compared with planets or asteroids, and its gravity is much stronger. If it were possible to stand on the fiery fields of its surface, a person would weigh 28 times more than on Earth.

But there are other objects in space with even greater forces of gravity than this. On the star Sirius B, a 12-year-old child might weigh over 20,000 tonnes. On a neutron star, such as that in the Crab Nebula, something as tiny as a grain of sand could weigh as much as 2,000 tonnes. (Neutron stars are super-dense objects left behind after massive stars have exploded.) The most powerful gravity is found on black holes, which are not really holes, but the densest objects in the universe.

Humans feel lighter on the Moon because it has less mass and weaker gravity than Earth. The Moon's gravity is about one-sixth as strong.

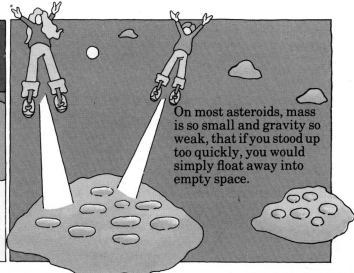

On most asteroids, mass is so small and gravity so weak, that if you stood up too quickly, you would simply float away into empty space.

The big bang

According to the 'Big Bang' theory, which is the one most generally accepted today, our universe began perhaps 9,000 to 15,000 million years ago, with a gigantic explosion. Some astronomers believe it was a super-dense, older universe which exploded, but there is no way we can know for certain.

For about a million years the universe was an expanding fireball of light. When it grew cooler, the first atoms formed. (An atom is the smallest unit of a chemical element. The first atoms created were those of hydrogen and helium.) Then gravity took over. It pulled together the small atomic particles within the great ball of gas and light. The material of the universe separated into billions of enormous clouds and, within these clouds, the stars were born.

The expanding universe

Thousands of millions of galaxies are still flying away from each other with the momentum of the first explosion. This means that our universe is still expanding.

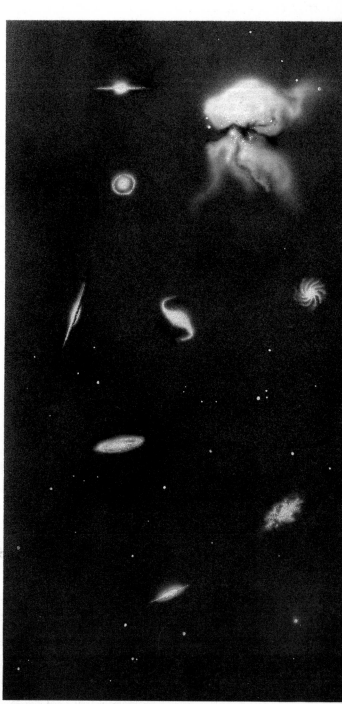

The temperature of the Big Bang is thought to have been many billions of degrees Centigrade. Galaxies of stars were created when gravity pulled together the dust and gas flying through space after the explosion.

As a result of the Big Bang, space is full of galaxies which are still flying away from each other at great speed

The rate of expansion in the universe can be calculated because of the Doppler Effect, a phenomenon named after Christian Doppler, the Austrian scientist who explained it.

The Doppler Effect

Sound alters its pitch as the source of the sound approaches us or moves away. The noise of a siren, for instance, is high as it approaches, then drops suddenly as the vehicle passes. Light behaves in a similar manner. When an object emitting light moves away from an observer, the light received shifts to the red end of the spectrum. This makes the star in a receding galaxy look redder. Astronomers call this phenomenon the Red Shift. Light waves of an approaching star shift to the blue end of the spectrum, so stars moving towards us look bluer.

Types of galaxies

Not all galaxies look the same. Basically, they take three forms: elliptical, irregular and spiral. Apart from our own Milky Way system, only three other galaxies are visible to the naked eye. They are M31 in the constellation of Andromeda and the two, irregular, Magellanic Clouds. M31, visible in the northern hemisphere, is a spiral galaxy about 2 million light years away.

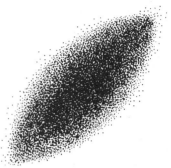

An elliptical galaxy is a group of stars in the neat shape of an ellipse. The stars are more closely packed at the middle.

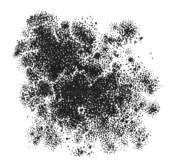

Irregular galaxies take no uniform shape. They lack the spiral form and the central bulge of galaxies like our own.

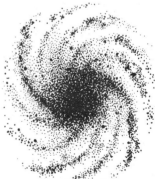

The spiral galaxy is a slowly-turning wheel of stars, with many stars in the 'arms'. From above, a spiral galaxy looks rather like a whirlpool.

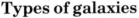

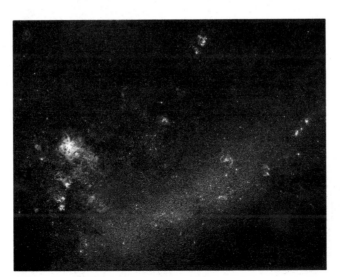

Several bright spherical shells of glowing gas are dotted among the 'bar' of central stars in the Large Magellanic Cloud, an irregular galaxy in the southern hemisphere.

Birth of stars

The process of creation which followed the Big Bang is still going on in the depths of space. Over millions of years, a vast dark cloud of gas and dust slowly contracts, rotates and pulls together under the influence of gravity, to form a star (a sun). Eventually, somewhere in the centre, the atoms become so closely packed that they frequently collide. This results in nuclear reactions, which generate energy. Light energy streams outwards, and the star is born.

Glowing clouds

Very hot new stars emit great quantities of ultraviolet light, a form which has such a short wavelength that it cannot be seen with the naked eye. This causes the nebula, or clouds of gas round the stars, to glow. If the material of the cloud is mainly hydrogen, it will glow with a reddish hue. The light from clouds of oxygen looks faintly green. These colours can be revealed in photographs of the nebula M42, which lies in the sword beneath Orion's belt.

Gas and dust left over after the formation of stars continues to be affected by the forces of gravitational attraction. It may settle down into a disc orbiting the central sun which has just been born. Then, by slow accumulation, all the matter could collect together to form planets. Our solar system was probably created in this way.

Other planetary systems

Even the largest telescopes cannot directly detect the faint objects circling other suns. But astronomers believe they are very common, and there is indirect evidence that several of the closest stars have planetary systems similar to our own.

Although we cannot see these planets, the paths which stars take through space can be plotted accurately by using a large telescope. A star with small planetary companions will be seen to wobble a little in its journey because the planets exert a slight gravitational pull on it. Barnard's star, which is close but faint, behaves in this way. It probably has two planets comparable in size to Jupiter.

The chance that life may exist on a few of these planets is good. Some astronomers cautiously estimate that there could be half-a-million planets in our own galaxy capable of supporting intelligent life.

Our solar system is so small a part of the universe, that someone on a star as close to us as Sirius, could not see the nine planets orbiting the Sun, even with the best man-made telescopes. Only the Sun's wobble would indicate that it had planetary companions.

The nebula M42 in the constellation of Orion, is still in turbulent motion. Within the clouds of glowing gas, which are millions of times bigger than our entire solar system, four new stars have recently been born.

A star's life

Once a star has settled down and begun its long life, it becomes one of a variety of types. Huge stars are called supergiants. Blue-white ones, such as Rigel, have surface temperatures of up to 30,000°C. Red supergiants, such as Betelgeuse, are cooler – about 3,000°C. At the other end of the scale are dwarfs. White ones are small and incredibly dense. Their matter is so tightly packed that a matchbox-full would weigh many tonnes. The star Sirius B is a white dwarf. It is smaller than the planet Uranus, but its mass almost equals that of our Sun. Red dwarfs, which are small and cool, are sometimes less than 1,000°C at the surface. They are so dim that we can see only a few of the nearest, even with the aid of a telescope.

The life cycle of our Sun

Between these extremes, our Sun is listed as a yellow 'G' type star. It has been in this 'stable' state for 5,000 million years, and will remain so for an equally long time in the future. Then, when all the hydrogen at the centre has been 'burned up', the Sun will become unstable and expand into a red giant. It will engulf the planet Mercury and scorch the surface of the Earth.

As a red giant, our Sun will burn fiercely for about 1,000 million years. Then its brightness will fade and it will begin to shrink, until it becomes a white dwarf – a star close to total extinction.

The Crab Nebula, a vast cloud of gas, is the debris of a supernova which was seen to explode in 1054. It was so bright that it was visible in daylight for two years. A neutron star at its centre spins 30 times per second.

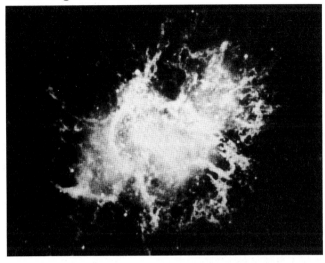

When the Sun expands, its heat will turn any remaining water to steam. Filling more than half our sky, it will blister, scorch and crack the Earth's surface. As the Sun grows cold, Earth will become a dark, frozen wasteland.

A few million years later, the Sun will shrink rapidly into a white dwarf, then slowly grow cold. It will end its life as a dark cinder known as a black dwarf.

Supernovas

A star whose mass is more than treble that of our Sun has a different life. Its internal nuclear processes become unstable, resulting in a gigantic explosion called a supernova. Most of the body of the star is flung out into space at almost 9,000 km per second. All that is left is a neutron star at the centre. This is a small, super-dense object which spins at tremendous speed.

Supernovas are rare. The last one visible in our galaxy was seen in 1604. The most famous supernova was observed in 1054. Photographs of that point in the sky reveal a cloud of gas and dust still splashing outwards from the explosion. It is the Crab Nebula, and it emits a spray of radio waves which flash at us like a lighthouse signal.

The black hole

With stars more than 10 times the mass of our Sun, there is no explosion. Instead, the star gets smaller and smaller. As its material is crushed tighter, its gravitational pull increases. The pull becomes so great that not even light can escape. Since the object cannot be seen, it is called a black hole. It has been suggested that many galaxies, including our own, may contain massive black holes at their centres.

Our galaxy

In the night sky, every separate star that can be seen with the naked eye, belongs to our galaxy. These are only a few of the 100,000 million stars that make up this typical spiral system. Through a telescope, swarms of distant suns can be seen in the ribbon of stars we call the Milky Way. Our galaxy is so enormous that light shining from a star on one side of it, travelling at 300,000 km per second, would take about 100,000 years to cross to the other side.

We see far more stars when we look towards the centre of our galaxy. The Milky Way is much brighter in that direction. (The galactic centre is hidden from us by clouds of interstellar dust, and it is possible that a giant black hole is located there, destroying stars that come too close.) The galaxy turns round its centre, but it is so large that it takes about 220 million years to make one complete revolution.

The brightness of stars

The Magnitude, or brightness of a star as it appears to us, depends upon two factors: its real brightness and its distance. The brightest stars – Sirius, Canopus and Alpha Centauri – are first Magnitude.

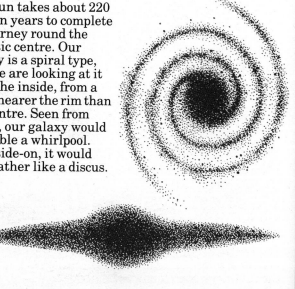

The Sun takes about 220 million years to complete its journey round the galactic centre. Our galaxy is a spiral type, and we are looking at it from the inside, from a point nearer the rim than the centre. Seen from above, our galaxy would resemble a whirlpool. Seen side-on, it would look rather like a discus.

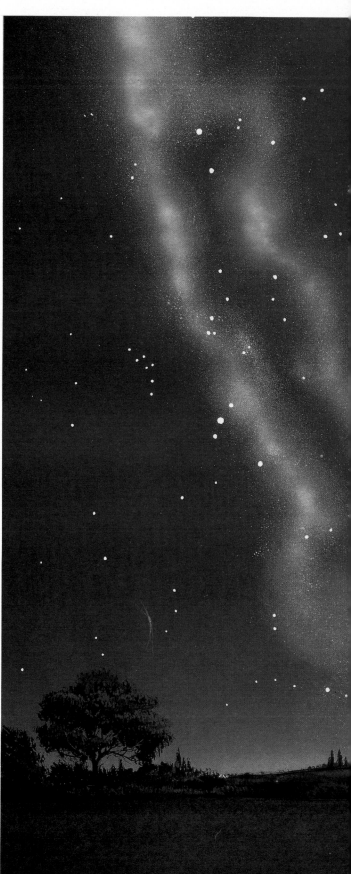

Part of our galaxy is called the Milky Way. To the naked eye, it appears as a faint ribbon of light running across the sky.

The faintest stars visible to keen eyes are sixth Magnitude. All the rest of the 'naked-eye' stars fall somewhere between the two. Although the brightest stars are not necessarily the closest, many stars are faint simply because they are far away. To compare stars accurately, there is a scale of Absolute Magnitude, which is a measure of the brightness which a star would have if it were placed 10 parsecs from Earth. (A parsec is 3.26 light years.)

Viewed from a space craft, most stars would appear as steady points of light. The twinkling that we see when we look from Earth is caused by our atmosphere. The turbulent air disturbs the rays of light, making the stars appear to flicker.

Pictures in the sky

All the stars which can be seen with the naked eye are divided up into constellations, or groups of stars. Most of the northern hemisphere constellations – such as Draco (the Dragon) – were named by astronomers of the Ancient World, who saw definite pictures in them. Those in the southern hemisphere – such as the Southern Cross – have been named much more recently.

The centre of our galaxy lies somewhere beyond the luminous star clouds and patches of dust in the constellation of Sagittarius.

The constellations

The names of some of the older constellations (Aries, Cancer, Leo, Libra and so on) are familiar to us because they are also the signs of the zodiac. The zodiac is the band of constellations through which the Sun appears to pass during the year. It spends about a month in each. The Moon orbiting the Earth and the planets orbiting the Sun also appear to move through these constellations.

Leo (the Lion) is one of the 12 constellations of the zodiac. Light from Regulus, the brightest star in the group, has been travelling towards Earth for 85 years.

When you look at a constellation, you are really gazing into the past down a kind of time tunnel. This is because the stars are at different depths in space, and the time taken for their light to reach us on Earth varies considerably. The four stars of the Southern Cross, for instance, vary in distance between 220 and 590 light years.

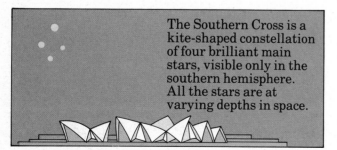

The Southern Cross is a kite-shaped constellation of four brilliant main stars, visible only in the southern hemisphere. All the stars are at varying depths in space.

One of the closest stars is Sirius, in the constellation of Canis Major (the Great Dog). Seen from Earth, it is the brightest star in our sky. Sirius is nine light years away, which means that you are seeing it as it was nine years ago.

Some stars are so bright that, although they are hundreds or even thousands of light years away, they can still be seen. Betelgeuse, 20,000 times brighter than our Sun, is visible at a distance of 650 light years. The star Deneb in the constellation of Cygnus (the Swan), is 1,600 light years away. It is also clearly visible because it is 60,000 times brighter than the Sun.

We are seeing Deneb, a first Magnitude star in Cygnus, as it was 1,600 years ago. This star is so bright that, despite its great distance, it is visible in our sky.

Compare these stellar distances with that of the Moon. From the Moon, reflected light takes only one-and-a-quarter seconds to reach Earth. Light from the street lamps of a town 10km distant travels to us in one-thirty-thousandth of a second!

Early astronomers thought that the stars were fixed in patterns, and so they appear to be. But it is only their great distances that make them look stationary. In 50,000 years' time, many star patterns will be unrecognisable because both the stars and our Earth will have moved so much. The Plough, for instance, will look completely different.

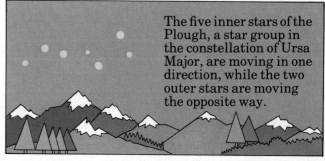

The five inner stars of the Plough, a star group in the constellation of Ursa Major, are moving in one direction, while the two outer stars are moving the opposite way.

If you watch the night sky regularly, you will learn to recognise the stars and constellations. The most spectacular star is Sirius, because it is the brightest. In the constellation of Orion, the blue-white star in Orion's right foot is Rigel. It is 815 light years away, but 50,000 times brighter than the Sun. The red star in Orion's shoulder is Betelgeuse.

Multiple stars

Clouds of interstellar dust reflect blue light from the Pleiades, a star cluster which looks like a swarm of fireflies.

Many of the stars in our galaxy, as well as those far out in space, are not simply lonely individuals. The majority of them belong to binary (double) or multiple star systems. To the naked eye, Castor, in the constellation of Gemini, looks like a single star. But Castor is a multiple system of three pairs of twin suns. The six stars are so close together that they cannot be distinguished separately, except with a telescope. Four of the stars are hot and blue, while the other two are cooler and red. A planet orbiting one of these pairs would have six coloured suns shining on it. Some astronomers think there is little chance of life evolving on such a planet, partly because of the extreme variations in temperature.

The winking demon

Algol, named 'the demon' by early Arabian astronomers, is a binary system. It is in the constellation of Perseus. The largest telescopes cannot detect the two stars separately, but we know about them because Algol 'winks', or dims in brightness, every few days. This happens when one star passes in front of the other and cuts off some of its light, so causing an eclipse. Several national newspapers give the times in the month when Algol 'winks' in this way.

Algol is called an eclipsing binary. Many other binaries can be detected only with a spectrograph, a special instrument which analyses light. These double stars are known as spectroscopic binaries.

Star clusters

Stars are also born in clusters, or groups. One of the loveliest is the Pleiades, on the shoulder of Taurus (the Bull). It is an open cluster of 200 stars. Keen eyes can pick out eight, and many more can be seen with the aid of binoculars.

Many clusters are not 'open' and irregular in shape, but are symmetrical and packed with up to a million suns. These are globular clusters. One, visible through binoculars in the northern hemisphere, is M13 in the constellation of Hercules. It lies deep in space, about 20,000 light years away, and has half-a-million suns. A planet orbiting one of these suns would never know the darkness of night – from horizon to horizon, the sky would constantly blaze with stars many times more brilliant than the brightest stars in our sky. Just in case there is anyone listening in M13, a radio message was beamed towards this cluster in 1972. The three-minute message, travelling at the speed of light, will take 20,000 years to arrive at its destination.

In a multiple system of six stars, an observer on this imaginary planet would sometimes see all six suns in the sky at once. Our Sun is a yellow star, but others may be almost any colour.

The Sun's family

Planet Earth is just one of a host of objects that circle the Sun. There are eight other planets, at least 32 moons, thousands of asteroids, countless comets and innumerable specks of dust. Many of the objects are visible to the naked eye.

Astronomers have known for thousands of years that the five bright 'naked-eye' planets (Mercury, Venus, Mars, Jupiter and Saturn) are different from the stars. They can be seen to move against the background of distant stars. Three outer planets – Uranus, Neptune and Pluto – are far too faint to follow with the naked eye, although two are giant planets.

The planets in motion

Seen from Earth, all the planets of our solar system appear to follow the same path across the sky, which runs through the 12 constellations of the zodiac. From Mars, planet Earth would seem to take the same route. Planets orbit the Sun in approximately the same plane. (Earth's plane is called the ecliptic.) In reality, they are like runners on a race circuit, some following inner tracks, others moving along outer ones.

The 'naked-eye' planets

Mercury, as it is so close to the Sun and never seen against an entirely dark sky, is the most elusive planet. It can only be seen just after sunset or just before sunrise.

Venus appears to us as the brightest of the planets. It dominates the sky at dawn or dusk, which is why it is often called the Morning or Evening Star. This planet shows phases like the Moon's, sometimes visible through a small telescope as a crescent.

Mars, at its closest to the Earth, is the second brightest planet and is distinguished from the rest by its reddish colour.

To the naked eye, Jupiter looks a little brighter than the brightest stars. Through binoculars, it appears as a cream-coloured object with four of its 14 moons visible.

Saturn has an incredible ring system. A small telescope is needed to see it clearly. Through binoculars, Saturn simply looks an odd shape. Some of the first observers, looking at it through poor-quality telescopes, thought the planet had handles!

Mercury Venus Earth Ma

It is rare to see all five 'naked-eye' planets at once. Sometimes four are visible. Mercury, Venus, Mars and Jupiter might look like this before sunrise in the northern hemisphere, or after sunset in the southern.

A small telescope, or even binoculars, will show that each of these 'naked-eye' planets has its own distinct image.

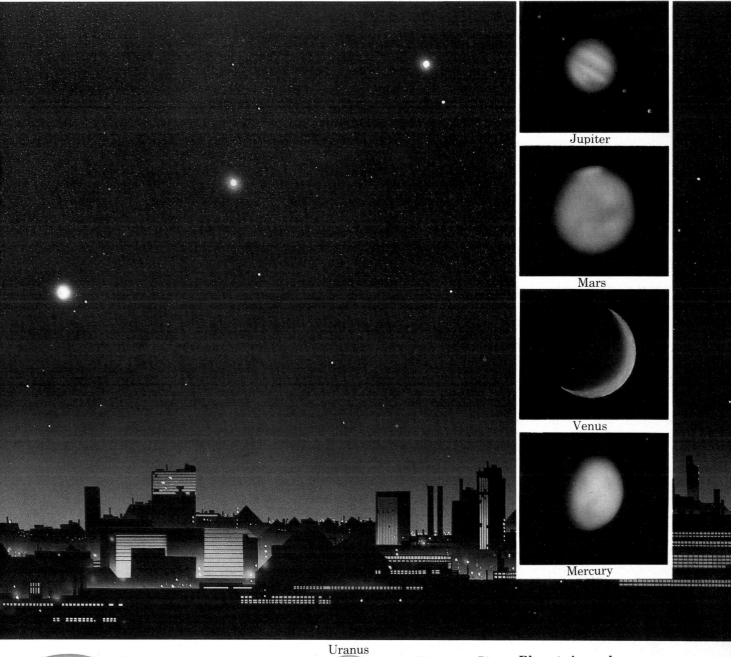

Jupiter

Mars

Venus

Mercury

Jupiter

Saturn

Uranus

Neptune

Pluto

Planets in scale
If the planets could be moved and put near each other, their relative sizes would become apparent. Jupiter would loom the largest, 11 times the diameter of Earth, but Mercury would be a tiny dot only a third the diameter of our planet.

Mercury and Venus

About 4,500 million years ago, rock 'rain' fell from the skies and moulded Mercury's scorched mountainous surface. In those early days, when space was still full of flying debris, these rocks were gigantic.

The hot cratered planet

Mercury is covered with craters as big as cities. Many of them have high, terraced walls and a mountain of compressed rock at their centres. The largest crater, the Caloris Basin, is 1,300 km in diameter and the mountains of its rim are 2km high.

Anyone standing on Mercury would need good protection. There is virtually no air, and the days are long and hot, with temperatures reaching 350°C. In the long nights, the temperature drops to −180°C.

Acid rain on Venus

A visitor would find a very different world on Venus. The Sun rises in the west and sets in the east, because the planet spins in a retro-grade direction (the opposite way to most planets). But sunrise could never be seen, because Venus is covered in thick clouds. The clouds and the rain contain sulphuric acid. The sky is full of thunderstorms, and lightning bolts illuminate the landscape.

Photographs of Mercury's surface, taken in 1974 by the space probe Mariner 10, proved the existence of craters similar to the Moon's.

Mercury is covered with vast craters caused by the impact of meteorites. Their presence was first revealed in 1972, when

NASA's Goldstone Deep Space station bounced radar waves off the planet's surface.

The atmosphere on Venus, which lets in heat from the Sun but does not let much out again, keeps the temperature around 500°C day and night. The top cloud layers scud round Venus in only four Earth-days, but there are no cooling breezes at the surface.

Pressure at ground level is nearly 100 times greater than on Earth. The first space probes, Venera 9 and 10, were crushed in a matter of minutes. To stand on the surface, an astronaut would need to be dressed like a deep-sea diver, in a suit strengthened to combat the pressure, with additional built-in protection against the heat.

Future life on Venus

One day we may be able to change the climate on Venus and make it less inhuman. Micro-organisms sent by rocket would breed rapidly, consuming the carbon dioxide which makes up 98% of the atmosphere, and breathing out oxygen. In theory, the clouds should then clear. The temperature and air pressure would drop, so improving the climate.

The light on Venus is a lurid red and visibility is only about 3km. Beyond that, the rock-strewn, cratered landscape is lost in murky gloom.

The Moon

In the highlands and mountainous regions of the Moon, much of the rock and rock dust looks like white plaster beneath the blazing Sun. Down on the solidified lava 'seas' (called maria), the dust is darker. These are soundless scenes because there is no air to carry sound waves. The Moon's many landslides happen in complete silence. In the weak gravity, thousands of tonnes of rock slip and bounce slowly to the base of a mountain, but an astronaut would be aware only of a tremor beneath his feet.

The single really colourful object in the whole scene is the Earth, hanging stationary in a black sky. It is blue and white, with patches of orange where there are deserts. The Moon itself is a great ball of rock, brilliantly lit by the Sun.

The Moon's orbit

We see varying amounts of the side of the Moon facing the Earth as it orbits our planet: half of it when the Sun is shining from one side, all of it at full Moon when the Sun shines from behind the Earth.

When the Moon passes exactly between the Earth and the Sun, it blocks our view of the Sun, causing a solar eclipse. A lunar eclipse occurs when the shadow of the Earth falls across the Moon.

We never see the far side of the Moon because gravity has locked it in its orbit so that one side always faces Earth, rather as dancers in a circle face inward.

Observing the Moon

The best time to observe our satellite with binoculars or a small telescope, is several days before full Moon. Mountains and craters stand out very clearly as they cast deep black shadows. Look at the Bay of Rainbows on the northern shore of the Sea of Rains. When sunlight first catches the mountain tops of the rim of this old, half-destroyed crater, the floor of the Bay is still shrouded in darkness.

At full Moon, you can see what are called rays. (Some of them are hundreds of kilometres long.) At least some of these are the whitish splashes of pulverised rock thrown out from impact craters such as Tycho.

The age of the Moon

We do not know whether the Earth and the Moon were formed together, or whether we captured the satellite at a later date. The cratered highlands were formed early in the Moon's history, about 4,600 million years ago. The solidified lava seas erupted from the interior at a later date, following the impact of asteroid-like bodies.

The rim and terraces of Eratosthenes, one of the thousands of craters on the near side of the Moon, can be seen with the aid of a small telescope.

The Tsiolkovskii crater, on the Moon's far side, was photographed by Russian space cameras. It has a carpet of lava and a central mountain.

All the features shown on this map of the Moon can be seen with binoculars. Most striking are the craters, which have been named after philosophers and scientists. The flat plains were once thought to be areas of water, and so were called 'seas'.

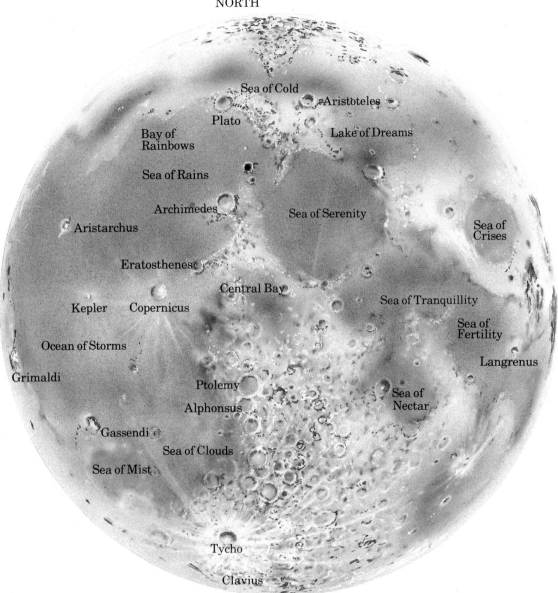

NORTH

Sea of Cold

Aristoteles

Plato

Lake of Dreams

Bay of Rainbows

Sea of Rains

Archimedes

Sea of Serenity

Aristarchus

Sea of Crises

Eratosthenes

Central Bay

Sea of Tranquillity

Kepler   Copernicus

Sea of Fertility

Ocean of Storms

Langrenus

Grimaldi

Ptolemy

Sea of Nectar

Alphonsus

Gassendi

Sea of Clouds

Sea of Mist

Tycho

Clavius

Plato's changing face
With binoculars, watch the crater of Plato over a month. When the Sun is rising on the Moon, the peaks round Plato's rim cast deep shadows. As the Sun rises in the Moon's sky, the shadows shorten. When the Sun sets, the shadows fall across Plato in the other direction.

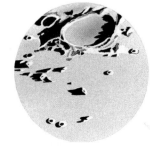

Plato, seen just after the Moon's first quarter.

The crater about four days before full Moon.

Plato, as seen in the Moon's last quarter.

Mars

The Martian day and night are almost exactly the same as Earth's. If you were there one sunrise, you might see an early morning mist hanging low over the rust-red desert. A light breeze and the warmth of the Sun would disperse it, although the temperature would not rise above −30°C. The air, which is 100 times thinner than on Earth, consists mostly of carbon dioxide.

Spectacular Martian scenery

Mars boasts the largest volcanoes and the most impressive canyon yet photographed in the solar system. The volcano Olympus Mons is almost three times the height of Mt Everest. The Valley of the Mariners is up to 6km deep and over 3,000 km long.

Like other planets with solid surfaces, Mars has many craters, although they are concentrated in the southern hemisphere. On other parts of the planet, there are large areas of piled-up sand dunes. At the poles, the ice caps are made of frozen carbon dioxide and water. They shrink in size during the Martian spring and summer, and are visible through a small telescope.

Rivers and canals

The most interesting features of all are the meandering valleys, which look like dried-up river beds. Perhaps rivers ran freely long ago, and great reserves of water may now lie frozen beneath the ground.

Earlier this century, it was thought that Mars was criss-crossed by a complex system of straight lines. It was even suggested that they were canals made by intelligent beings. But there are no canals. People simply imagined them.

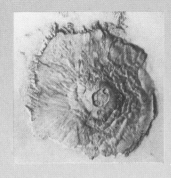

Space probes Viking I and II, which soft-landed on Mars in 1976, found no conclusive signs of life. But their photographs showed some exciting features. One is Olympus Mons, a gigantic volcano which may be the largest in our solar system.

Many people have wondered whether life existed on Mars when the planet had water. No evidence of life was found by the two Viking craft which landed gently on the surface of Mars in 1976. But, since the discovery of two oases of dampness just south of the Martian equator, some scientists are questioning the Viking evidence.

Satellites of Mars

Mars has two moons – Phobos (Fear) and Deimos (Panic). They are only a few kilometres across and orbit the planet rapidly in seven-and-a-half and 30 hours respectively. They might be captured asteroids. Close-up photographs show that their surfaces are pock-marked with craters.

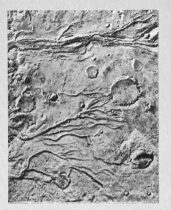

Both Viking craft were amazingly sophisticated. Viking I landed smoothly on Chryse Planitia (the Gold Plain), a lowland area where water probably once flowed. There, it collected and analysed soil and rocks, and took hundreds of photographs.

The Martian sky is pink, due to high-flying dust from the desert and the occasional sandstorm. The horizon seems closer than on Earth because Mars is only half our size.

Smaller companions

A number of asteroids, meteors and comets belong to our solar system. The majority of asteroids orbit the Sun in a belt between Mars and Jupiter, although some – Chiron, for instance – lie far beyond Jupiter.

Asteroids

Eros, a typical asteroid, is a ragged hunk of rock 14km long. Asteroids are probably fragments of small planets which kept colliding with each other. There are about 100,000 asteroids, ranging from the size of a house to that of a minor planet. The largest, Ceres, has a diameter of 760 km.

More than 2,000 asteroids have been identified, but only Vesta is faintly visible to the naked eye. Some asteroids swing as close to the Sun as Mercury, and Icarus, a huge boulder, has been known to pass quite close to Earth. Every million years at least one small flying mountain will crash on Earth, causing an enormous crater.

Meteors and meteor showers

Meteors, or shooting stars, are tiny grains of matter which travel faster than a rifle bullet and disintegrate when they enter Earth's atmosphere. When they are 80km above ground, their speed causes the thin air to glow, which we see as a bright, brief 'tail'.

Meteorites, generally, are lumps of stone or iron which survive the fall from space. They are easy to see against the ice and snow at the poles.

Meteors are flashes of light made as tiny grains of matter streak across the sky. They are visible on most clear nights.

A bright comet such as this appears about every 10 years. The comet only grows a tail as it approaches the Sun.

Some meteors are called sporadic because the times at which they appear are unpredictable. Meteor showers, however, can be predicted and seen on certain nights. When Earth is passing through a meteor swarm (which may be the trail of a disintegrating comet), meteors seem to shoot out from one part of the sky. This is called their radiant. One of the best meteor showers is the Perseids, visible on August 13. All the meteors appear to fly from the radiant of the constellation of Perseus, hence their name.

Comets

Comets have been described as giant, dirty snowballs. They have a small nucleus (possibly of rock particles), frozen in water and ammonia, surrounded by a vast halo of dust and gas. The tails which some comets grow may be millions of kilometres in length.

Many comets swing round the Sun once, then sweep off into deep space, never to be seen again. Others maintain elliptical orbits that make them return regularly to our sky. Halley's comet, which was last seen in 1910, returns every 76 years.

As a comet orbits the Sun, the solar wind and the pressure of sunlight cause dust and gas in the comet to stream away like a great tail. The tail generally points away from the Sun.

Jupiter

If Jupiter had been bigger it might have become a star. But Jupiter is not quite massive enough for the nuclear reactions to begin which would cause it to shine by its own light. Even so, Jupiter is 318 times more massive than the Earth.

Lightning bolts and hydrogen seas

Jupiter has no solid surface. What we see in photographs are the cold tops of great swirling clouds of ammonia, in a dense atmosphere of mainly hydrogen and methane. Somewhere deep down in the gloomy darkness, lit irregularly by vivid flashes of super-bolts of lightning, is a dark and stormy sea of liquid hydrogen. There, even if you had a boat and could survive the crushing pressure, you would weigh about two-and-a-half times your normal weight.

Although the top layers of cloud are at the freezing temperature of −150°C, it is an intriguing speculation that, deeper in the atmosphere where it is warmer, life might have developed. All the right elements needed to make amino acids – the first building bricks of life – exist there. The energy to create them could come from a lightning bolt. Whether any simple life forms could survive long enough to evolve into other forms, is another question.

Jupiter's moons

Most of the smaller of Jupiter's 14 moons are probably captured asteroids. The four largest – Io, Ganymede, Europa and Callisto – are visible through binoculars. Ganymede and Callisto, each bigger than our Moon, are virtually giant snowballs. Their surfaces are covered with cracks, ridges and craters, all sculpted in icy material. Europa, which is a little smaller, has a thick frozen crust round its rocky core. Io is a very different place. In 1972, when the Voyager I space craft photographed Io for the first time, there were several active volcanoes.

Looking out from Io

From Io, Jupiter would appear enormous and very beautiful. Orange, yellow, red and grey-blue clouds would change their patterns day by day while the planet spun rapidly on its axis. The Great Red Spot would be clearly visible, rising through the clouds.

Jupiter's Great Red Spot is larger than the Earth and may be a giant storm. The eddies of wavy lines are disturbed areas in the cloud belt, caused by the Red Spot and other storm centres travelling at different speeds round the planet.

Europa, one of Jupiter's 14 moons (left), was photographed by Voyager II in 1972. Between its icy crust and the core, may lie an ocean where life could exist.

With its swirling clouds and its Great Red Spot, Jupiter would be a spectacular sight from Io, one of its moons. Io itself is volcanic. Its surface is encrusted with sulphur flows, salts and bluish-white icy material.

Saturn

Saturn's 10 moons orbit beyond the rings. Titan, which is slightly larger than Mercury, has its own atmosphere.

The most amazing feature of Saturn is its beautiful ring system. The rings are not solid sheets, but made up of billions of separate lumps of rock and ice which orbit the planet. These lumps may be no bigger than snowballs and pebbles. We know this because radar waves have been bounced off the rings and the echo analysed by astronomers.

Wafer-thin rings

Although the diameter of Saturn's outer ring is 272,000 km, none of the rings is more than about 10km thick. As Saturn orbits the Sun, we see the rings from different angles. In 1980 they were edge-on to us, and visible only through the largest telescopes as a wafer-thin line.

An accurate measurement of the density of each ring and its diameter was made in 1977. The light from Iapetus, one of Saturn's moons, was observed as it dimmed and brightened when passing behind the ring system. This event is called an occultation.

Of the rings, the two main ones are most easily distinguishable. They are separated by the Cassini Division, a 4,000-km gap which is relatively free of particles. (The space craft Pioneer II found that the Division does contain some.) The gravitational pull of Mimas, a moon orbiting beyond the rings, has the effect of regularly sweeping the gap almost clean, as particles are made to fall either into the outer or the inner of the two main rings.

No one knows how the rings were formed. They may be the debris of a moon, pulled to pieces by the planet's gravity. Or the particles may have been too close to the planet to come together into one object.

Saturn's surface

There can be no hope of landing on Saturn. Like Jupiter, although somewhat smaller, it is a great ball of gas and liquid hydrogen. At its centre, beneath thousands of kilometres of metallic hydrogen, the planet has a very small, rocky core.

Saturn, the most distant planet that can be seen with the naked eye, is a planetary giant – about 119,300 km in diameter. Like Jupiter, it spins rapidly and its surface is gaseous. But Saturn's most remarkable feature is its ring system. The rings extend outwards for 81,000 km, yet individual rings are probably no more than 10km thick.

The outer planets

Beyond Saturn are three more planets – Uranus, Neptune and Pluto. There are also innumerable comets and probably several asteroids. So far, only one asteroid has been discovered. It was first observed in 1977, and has been named Chiron.

Gaseous planets

Uranus and Neptune are giant planets of gas, similar to Saturn and Jupiter and several times larger than the Earth.

Uranus was discovered in 1781 by William Herschel, when he realised that what he thought was a star had moved. Astronomers of the time were surprised, as they thought Saturn was the outermost planet.

Uranus appears to have a system of five rings. They are very faint and were only discovered in 1977, when observers were watching the planet as it passed in front of a distant star. The starlight dimmed five times as Uranus approached. Later, as it moved away, the same thing happened. As well as the five rings, Uranus has five moons.

Neptune was discovered in 1846, when astronomers turned their telescopes to the position predicted by two brilliant mathematicians, Englishman John Adams and the Frenchman, Urbain le Verrier. They simultaneously worked out that the slightly irregular orbit of Uranus must be caused by the gravitational pull of another planet.

Pluto, the coldest planet

Computers are now being used to investigate another planetary problem. Pluto, which was not discovered until 1930, has a very odd orbit. Sometimes it crosses the orbit of

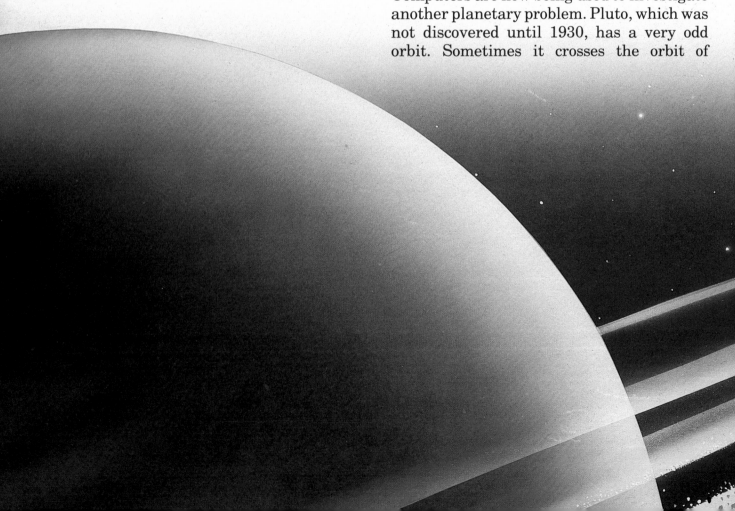

Pluto is a cold and dark planet. It's surface may be covered in some icy material, or with pools of liquid methane.

Neptune, so coming closer to the Sun than that planet. One theory is that Pluto was once a moon of Neptune. Long ago, a planet-sized object may have swept through the solar system, dragging Pluto away from Neptune and leaving it to wander a solitary course round the Sun.

Pluto is an inhospitable place, with no atmosphere and a surface temperature of perhaps $-230°C$. This is close to Absolute Zero $(-273°C)$, which makes Pluto one of the coldest places in the universe. The planet is probably icy in composition. It is too far away to receive much warmth from the Sun. In fact, from Pluto, the Sun would be simply a bright light in a star-studded sky.

Uranus has five rings of gas, dust and rocks. The planet's surface is hidden by a mantle of greenish methane gas.

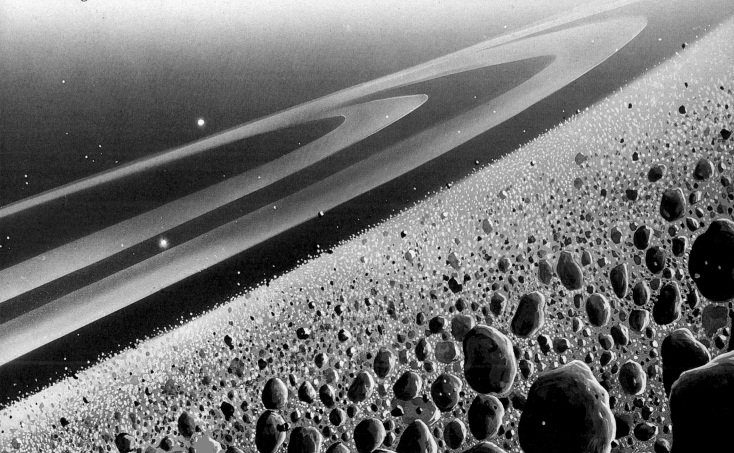

The future

Within the next few years, astronomers hope to have a large telescope in orbit above the Earth's atmosphere. Such a telescope could probe so many light years into space that it would be looking back in time almost to the moment of the Big Bang.

A fundamental question about the universe is whether or not it will go on expanding forever. Some astronomers think that there is enough material in the universe to slow down the expansion by the pull of gravity, and reverse it, so that everything will fall back together into something like a giant black hole.

Space colonies

Perhaps the most significant development within the next few years will be the colonisation of space. It is bound to happen, as we already have the knowledge and technical ability to achieve it.

One of the most favoured plans is for the construction of giant cylinders which could house hundreds of thousands of people in a natural environment. Built from materials mined on the Moon, or perhaps even on asteroids, the cylinder would spin slowly and so create artificial gravity – on the same principle that water stays in a bucket if you swing it very rapidly over your head.

Life in the universe

Although we have not found life anywhere else within our solar system, it may well have developed on planets orbiting other suns. There may be thousands of advanced civilisations in our own galaxy – and that is only a small part of the total universe.

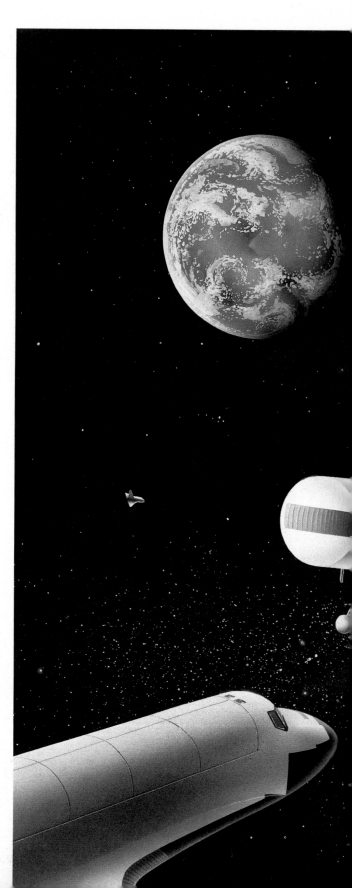

Life in a space cylinder would be just like life on Earth. By altering the angle of mirrors over the windows, the inhabitants would enjoy an illusion of day, night and the four seasons. Small cylinders would be used for farming and industry.

Charting the sky

Statistics of our solar system

Sun's diameter
1,392,000 km

	Mercury	Venus	Earth	Mars	Jupiter	Saturn	Uranus	Neptune	Pluto
Average distance from the Sun in millions of km	58	108	150	228	778	1,427	2,870	4,497	5,999
Diameter in km	4,880	12,104	12,756	6,787	142,200	119,300	51,800	49,500	3,000(?)
Length of year in Earth-days	0.24	0.62	1	1.88	11.9	29.5	84	165	249
Average surface temperature	350°C (day) −180°C (night)	500°C	22°C	−30°C	−150°C	−180°C	−210°C	−220°C	−230°C(?)
Number of moons	0	0	1	2	14	10	5	2	1(?)

The 15 brightest stars in the northern and southern hemispheres

Name of the star	Name of its constellation	Distance in light years	Description of the star
Sirius	Canis Major	8.7	White, with a white dwarf companion
Canopus	Carina	180	Yellow giant
Alpha Centauri	Centaurus	4.3	Multiple system of three stars
Arcturus	Boötes	36	Red giant, as bright as 100 Suns
Vega	Lyra	26	White, as bright as 50 Suns
Rigel	Orion	815	Blue giant, as bright as 50,000 Suns
Capella	Auriga	45	Binary system of two yellow giants
Procyon	Canis Minor	11	Yellow, with a white dwarf companion
Achernar	Eridanus	142	Blue, as bright as 200 Suns
Beta Centauri	Centaurus	400	Blue-white, as bright as 10,000 Suns
Altair	Aquila	16	White
Aldebaran	Taurus	68	Red giant, 40 times the diameter of the Sun
Acrux	Southern Cross	270	Blue-white double star
Betelgeuse	Orion	650	Red supergiant, as bright as 20,000 Suns
Antares	Scorpio	400	Red supergiant, with a smaller green companion

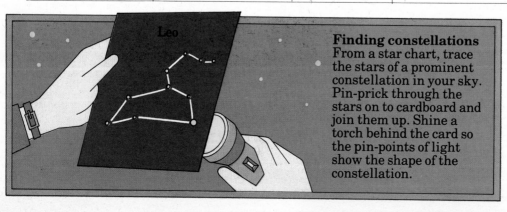

Finding constellations
From a star chart, trace the stars of a prominent constellation in your sky. Pin-prick through the stars on to cardboard and join them up. Shine a torch behind the card so the pin-points of light show the shape of the constellation.

Looking for meteors
Meteor showers appear to come from one point in the sky. The best nights to look are: January 4, Quadrantids (Boötes); April 19-22, Lyrids (Lyra); July 27-August 17, Perseids (Perseus); October 15-25, Orionids (Orion); November 14-17, Leonids (Leo); December 9-13, Geminids (Gemini).

Index

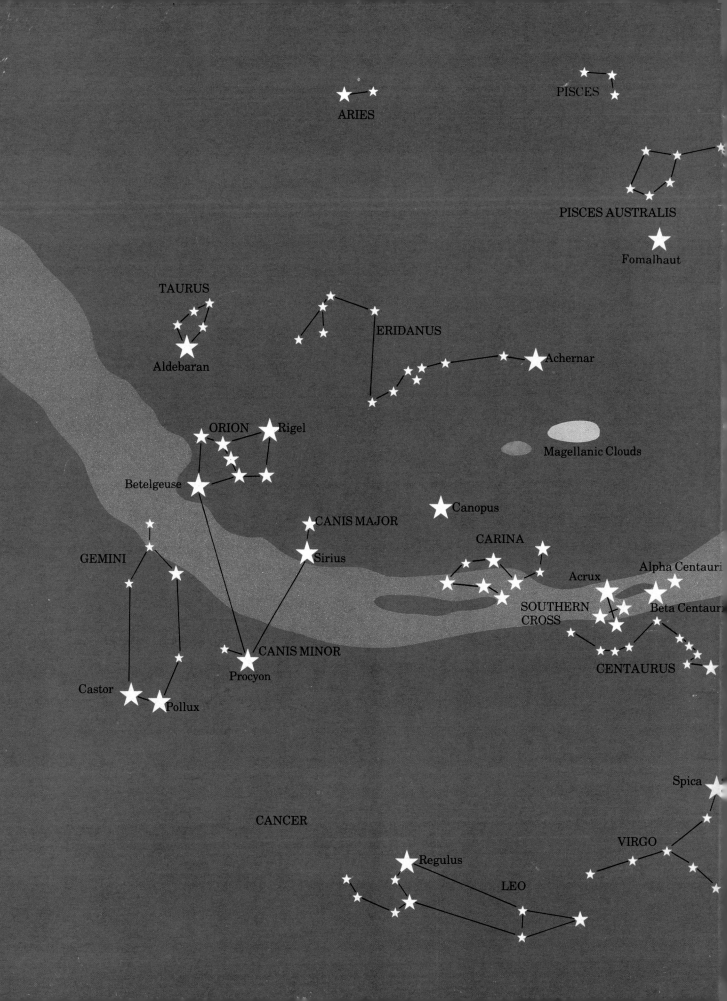

ARIES

PISCES

PISCES AUSTRALIS

Fomalhaut

TAURUS

ERIDANUS

Achernar

Aldebaran

Magellanic Clouds

ORION   Rigel

Betelgeuse

Canopus

CANIS MAJOR

CARINA

Sirius

Alpha Centauri

GEMINI

Acrux

SOUTHERN
CROSS   Beta Centauri

CANIS MINOR

CENTAURUS

Castor

Procyon

Pollux

Spica

CANCER

VIRGO

Regulus

LEO